Fantastic Lives

Business Sense

Michelle R. Prather, M.A.

Publishing Credits

Rachelle Cracchiolo, M.S.Ed., *Publisher*
Conni Medina, M.A.Ed., *Managing Editor*
Nika Fabienke, Ed.D., *Series Developer*
June Kikuchi, *Content Director*
John Leach, *Assistant Editor*
Evan Ferrell, *Graphic Designer*

TIME and the TIME logo are registered trademarks of TIME Inc. Used under license.

Image Credits: front cover, p.29, p.30, Courtesy of Margaret Pattillo; p.4 (bottom) Sergei Bachlakov/Shutterstock; pp.6–7, p.8, p.9, p.11 Courtesy of MAX'IS Creations, Inc.; p.10 (bottom) Oleksiy Naumov/Shutterstock; pp.12–13, pp.14–15, pp.16–17, pp.18–19, pp.40–41 Courtesy of Empower Orphans; p.15 (bottom) Nieboer/PPE/SIPA/Newscom; p.22 Paul Christian Gordon/Zuma Press/Newscom; p.23, pp.24–25, pp.26–27 Courtesy of iRummage; p.28, p.31 (top) Courtesy of Mr. Cory's Cookies; p.31 (bottom) Featureflash Photo Agency/Shutterstock; p.32, p.33 Doug Meszler/Splash News/Newscom; pp.34–35, pp.36–37, pp.38–39 Courtesy of Kidzcationz; all other images from iStock and/or Shutterstock.

All companies and products mentioned in this book are registered trademarks of their respective owners or developers and are used in this book strictly for editorial purposes; no commercial claim to their use is made by the author or the publisher.

Library of Congress Cataloging-in-Publication Data

Names: Prather, Michelle Rene?e, 1975- author.
Title: Fantastic lives : business sense / Michelle R. Prather.
Description: Huntington Beach, CA : Teacher Created Materials, [2019] | Includes index.
Identifiers: LCCN 2017058484 | ISBN 9781425850043 (pbk.)
Subjects: LCSH: Businesspeople--Juvenile literature. | Entrepreneurship--Juvenile literature. | Success in business--Juvenile literature.
Classification: LCC HC29 .P73 2019 | DDC 658.1/1--dc23
LC record available at https://lccn.loc.gov/2017058484

Teacher Created Materials

5301 Oceanus Drive
Huntington Beach, CA 92649-1030
www.tcmpub.com

ISBN 978-1-4258-5004-3

© 2019 Teacher Created Materials, Inc.

Table of Contents

Great Minds 4

Max Ash 6

Neha Gupta 12

Belle Pan 22

Cory Nieves 28

Bella Tipping 34

The Takeaway 40

Glossary 42

Index 44

Check It Out! 46

Try It! 47

About the Author 48

Great Minds

Do you want to know something truly **empowering**? There is no age requirement when it comes to having a brilliant idea. Transforming a concept into a success story isn't just for tech and corporate giants. Anyone can brainstorm an innovative way to make the world better. But people who have business sense often share a few essential characteristics. They pay attention to the world around them, are often creative, know how to solve problems, and are good at seeing things through.

The young people featured in this book possess a blend of these qualities—and more. These **entrepreneurs** saw needs and used their imaginations to create opportunities. After bringing their ideas to **fruition**, they all found ways to give back to their communities. And they've done it all while studying and, well, just being kids. Read on to learn about their compelling and inspirational stories.

Are You Savvy?

When you are savvy about something, you know how to do it well. It means you use your knowledge to help you know what to do. When you are business savvy, you use your instincts to guide you in business.

Max Ash

Have you ever heard the saying "Imitation is the **sincerest** form of flattery"? Well, when Max Ash was eight, he learned that when your friends try to copy your idea, maybe you're onto something.

In 2012, the Boston-area student was crafting a mug in art class when a stroke of creative genius struck him: Why not add a basketball hoop to the back of the mug? There's no better way to get marshmallows into a mug of hot chocolate! Ash, an **avid** sports fan, went with his instincts and did just that. Then, other kids added hoops on their mugs, too.

A Slam Dunk

Ash's parents listened to him when he told them about the popularity of his idea. He told them that he might want to turn it into a business. They contacted local experts and family friends to help get the ball rolling.

Ash's original mug

MAX'IS Creations

Ash came up with the company name himself. It speaks volumes about him, his creativity, and **dyslexia**. When said aloud, it sounds like "Max's Creations." But it also communicates another idea: "Max is creations."

Patent-Protected

Whether they are classmates or business competitors, other people cannot lay claim to Ash's ingenious concept now. He has been granted patents for his collection of sports-themed mugs. That means the U.S. government has given Ash the sole right to make and sell his inventions in the United States.

Ash's father found a local engineering consultant to make a 3-D **prototype** of his mug. After that, what is now known as The Mug With A Hoop® enjoyed a string of wins. The first win occurred when a professor of entrepreneurship at a nearby university invited Ash to present his idea. Then, Ash entered a product **pitch** contest. To his surprise, he was one of the 10 finalists chosen to pitch their ideas at Fenway Park in Boston!

Ash pitches his ideas at Fenway Park.

Role Playing

Ash's official role is Chief Creator, and the job takes a lot of time and work. He answers interview questions, makes product videos, and plays a key part in making sure his mugs are manufactured to a high standard. When it's time to wind down, he likes to play basketball and baseball—and he loves video games!

Making a Name

Soon, a lot of people knew about Ash and his mug. Local newspapers, websites, and blogs featured stories about him. When interest grows, it's a great time to raise money. So Ash launched a **crowdfunding** campaign online for his business and the research program at his school, which helps with language-based learning differences. He ended up exceeding the fundraising goal he set.

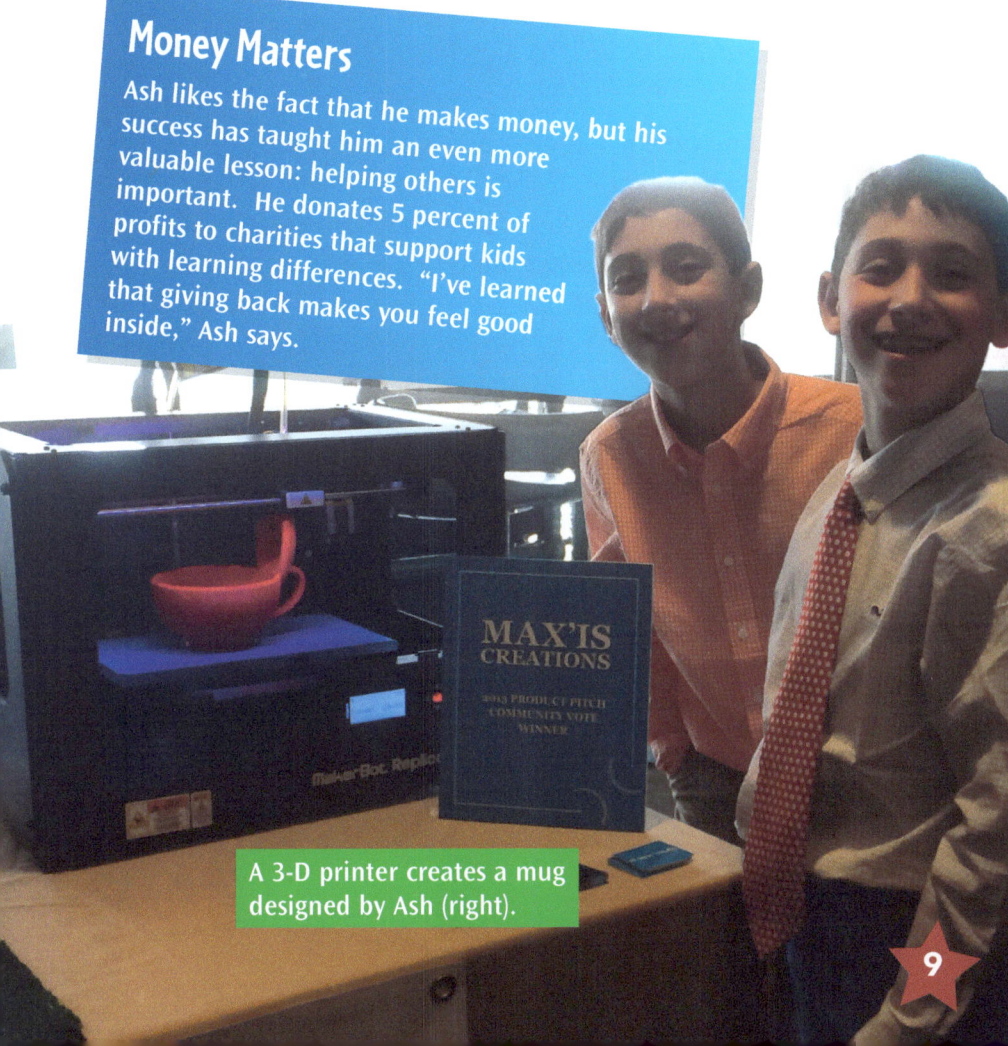

Money Matters

Ash likes the fact that he makes money, but his success has taught him an even more valuable lesson: helping others is important. He donates 5 percent of profits to charities that support kids with learning differences. "I've learned that giving back makes you feel good inside," Ash says.

A 3-D printer creates a mug designed by Ash (right).

"I Want to Keep Going"

Running your own business is hard work. When MAX'IS Creations started in 2012, Ash looked for people to invest in his company. Many people turned him down and told him that the business would likely lose money. But Ash kept going. Ash and his family have talked many times about whether they should keep going with the business. Ash's answer is always the same: he doesn't want to quit. It's a good thing, too, because he sold more than 65,000 mugs between 2014 and 2017. They are on sale at several shops online, at Nordstrom, and even at the Basketball Hall of Fame.

Ash doesn't quit when it comes to other challenges either, such as living with dyslexia. "Reading is still a struggle for me sometimes. Reading to myself is easier, but reading out loud is harder, and comprehension is the hardest," he says. "My advice for other kids is to keep working at it because it helps you in life."

Hero Status

Ash looks up to Kevin Durant. The basketball star may be famous for his impressive skills on the court, but he also runs his own charity to aid at-risk youth. Durant has surprised many fans by coming to visit them in the hospital.

Ash, his brother, and his father with his mugs

THINK LINK

Ash is an excellent entrepreneur in part because having dyslexia has taught him to persevere. He also has grown to be more business minded. Let's explore the entrepreneurial mindset further.

> Starting a business can feel like an uphill battle. How do you think a person with business sense deals with challenges?

> Do you think successful entrepreneurs make decisions and achieve goals on their own, as part of a team, or a combination of the two? How?

> In what ways does being creative make someone a stronger entrepreneur?

Neha Gupta

A family birthday tradition helped shape Neha Gupta's view of the world. To show gratitude for another year of life and good fortune, Gupta and her family would travel from the United States to their hometown in India to deliver food and gifts to orphans. Gupta was just nine years old when she realized how serious the orphans' situation was. They lacked basic resources, and they weren't going to school. This harsh reality changed Gupta forever.

Taking Action

Gupta was so moved that she organized a garage sale at her home. With the earnings, she purchased books, sweaters, and food for the orphans for the following Christmas. The kids welcomed her family back to India by putting up a decorated tree and performing a dance. The experience inspired Gupta to keep helping, and it laid the **groundwork** for what would become Empower Orphans.

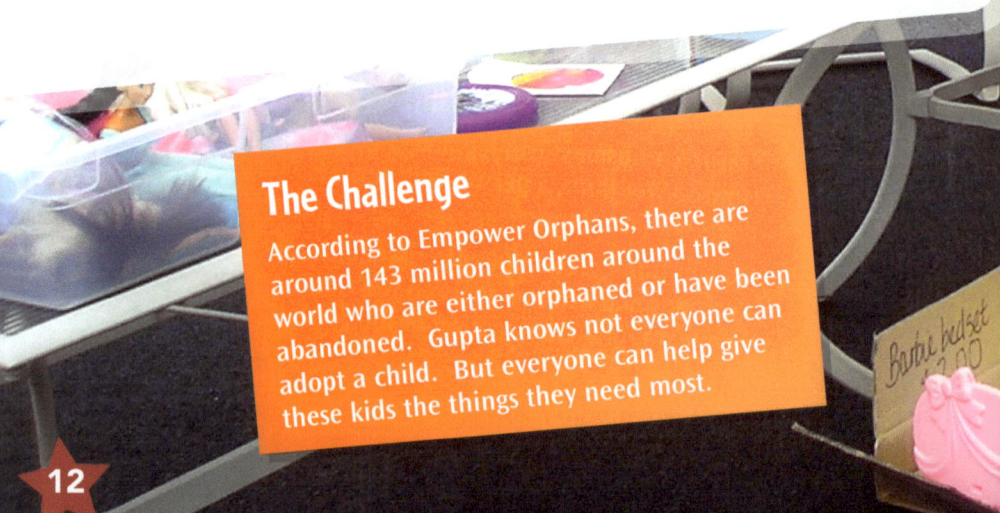

The Challenge

According to Empower Orphans, there are around 143 million children around the world who are either orphaned or have been abandoned. Gupta knows not everyone can adopt a child. But everyone can help give these kids the things they need most.

Magic Moment

As the Christmas visit to the orphanage came to a close, a girl approached Gupta and embraced her warmly. "She said, 'Thank you for being there for us,'" recalls Gupta. "It was that small gesture that made me appreciate the smallest things in life and got me hooked on service."

Gupta's first fundraiser

The Rewards of Work

Empower Orphans was formally established in 2009. So far, the nonprofit organization has raised more than $2 million in cash and **in kind**. The money is used for antipoverty and educational services throughout the United States, India, Central and South America, and Haiti. Gupta raised a large portion of the money on her own. Besides selling her toys, she has also sold homemade wine glass charms and has gone door-to-door to ask for donations.

Call to Action

Gupta has received many awards, and most recognize that she both helps and inspires kids. "I try to relate vulnerable children's experiences to peers with **empathy**," she says. "The goal is to make them understand the situation and then convert their empathy into action."

Now, the impact of her vision has gone far beyond what she first imagined. Volunteers, who run their own fundraisers through the Empower Orphans website and Facebook, make this happen. Kids in need have received new libraries, computer centers, and science labs. Other kids now have clean water and eye clinics, and the list goes on. And that's how Gupta, now an adult, wants it.

Gupta visits a school in India.

Great Honor

Gupta won the International Children's Peace Prize in 2014. She was the first American to receive it. Two important people presented the award to Gupta. One person was the Dutch king Willem-Alexander (left). The other was Desmond Tutu, who won the Nobel Peace Prize in 1984.

The Business of Giving

Running a charity is a labor of love. It isn't about how much money you bring in; it's about making an impact. Raising funds for a charity requires hard work and persistence. Empower Orphans, based in Pennsylvania where Gupta lives, relies on volunteers to raise funds for important services. If volunteers lose steam or drop off, then moving forward with programs becomes incredibly difficult. Gupta says that fundraising is an ongoing challenge, especially when her charity is "growing faster than you have the **manpower** to handle."

The amount of media attention Gupta has received has helped drive involvement. In 2015, she was chosen for a Microsoft advertising campaign that featured students working to improve the world. A video that included Gupta's story was shown in movie theaters and on social media. The response was remarkable.

Looking Forward

Empower Orphans has made great **strides**, expanding health camps in India. The camps treat illnesses and offer wellness checkups and critical vaccinations. Gupta wants to open more health camps around the world.

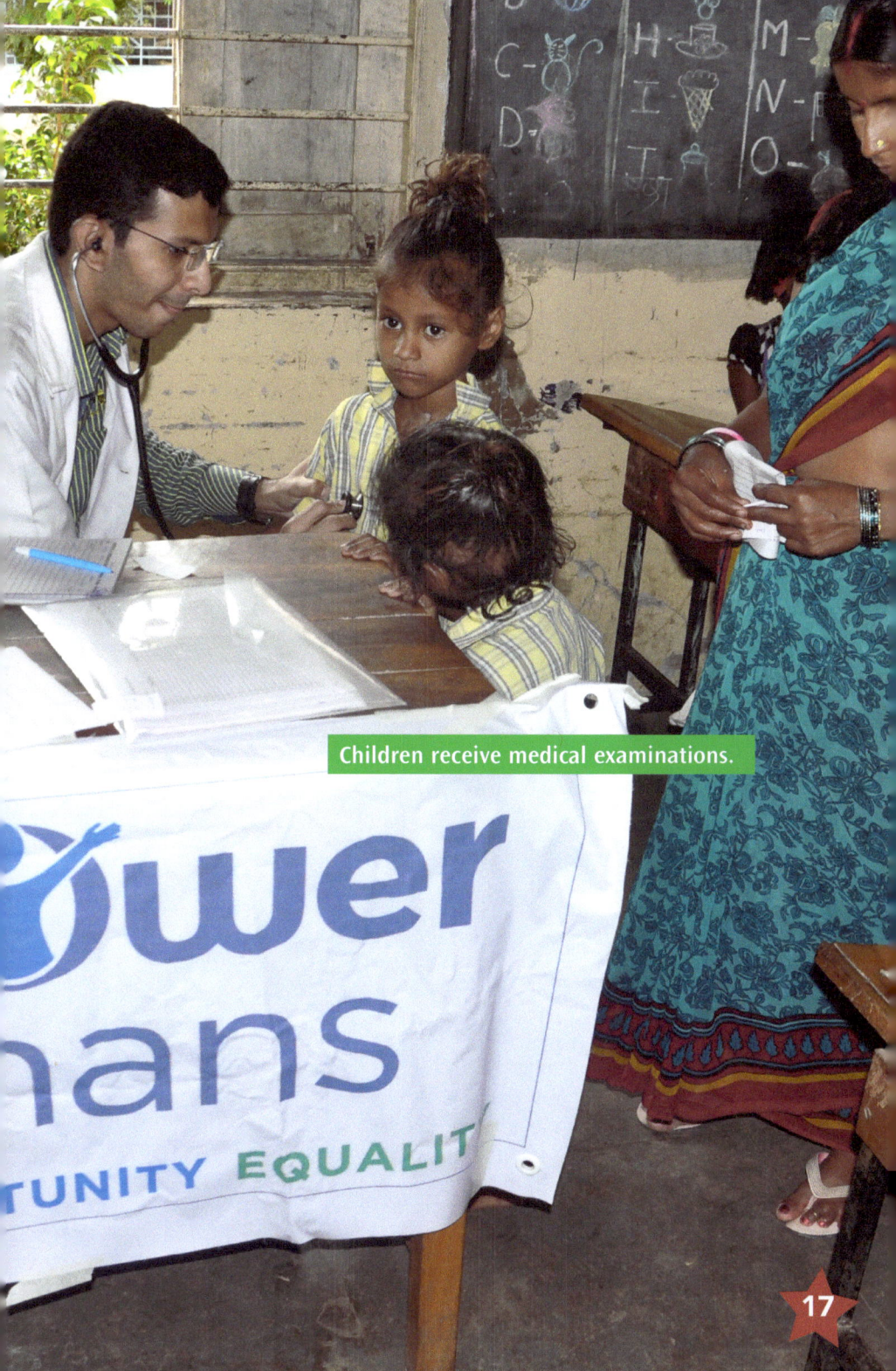
Children receive medical examinations.

An Education

Many orphans do not have the supplies they need to go to school. So Gupta and her volunteers raise money to provide items such as shoes, books, and book bags to orphanages. Doing this for years makes Gupta grateful for what she has. "It has made me appreciate privileges, like education and health care," she says. "[It has] shaped my passion to be a doctor, made me an **advocate** for children's rights, and made me a confident public speaker. From such a young age, I have had to interact with people from different age groups. This has certainly shaped my personality."

It's a wonder she can balance it all. She isn't overwhelmed by school and extracurricular activities. She says that when the extra things you take on uplift you, they don't feel like extra work.

Time to Heal

One month into her first year at Pennsylvania State University, Gupta fell and was injured. She suffered a brain injury. She had to take a long break from school and undergo rehab to fully recover. She worked hard to recover so that she could keep helping others.

Head Start

A poll revealed that more than three-fourths of kids from grades 5 to 12 wanted to be their own bosses. Nearly half wanted to either start their own businesses or create world-changing inventions. In the last several years, business-minded kids have gained considerable notoriety. If you want to be president of your own company, check out a few types of businesses you could start.*

Green Business

These businesses are intended to help the environment, and running one shouldn't hurt it. Think earth-friendly beauty products or organic food services. Or consider an **upcycled** fashion line or furniture repair shop. You could even fix up old bikes.

Online Business

You don't need to rent space to sell your goods. You just need a domain name, a web host, and a website that draws in people. And you don't need to invest in costly advertising. Instead, you can get creative and reach customers through social media.

You-Based Business

This is another form of online business. Countless "regular" kids have gained fame online. If you have something positive to share with the world, try creating a blog or a podcast. These have the potential to earn money through advertising.

*There are rules and regulations for starting a business. Be sure to research them carefully.

Belle Pan

As a new student, Belle Pan realized that her Seattle school's annual fundraising rummage sale, which was over 60 years old, was no longer thriving. In fact, running it had become a lot of work. She decided to find a solution. So she worked with her entrepreneur father, JT Pan, to help thrust the program into the modern age.

Big Idea

The first step was to come up with a way to sell used items and then transfer the profit directly to schools instead of a personal bank account. The father-and-daughter team put their heads together to research and design a model for an app that would fit the bill. Little did Pan know that soon she would be pitching the idea at a large start-up event she and her father attended.

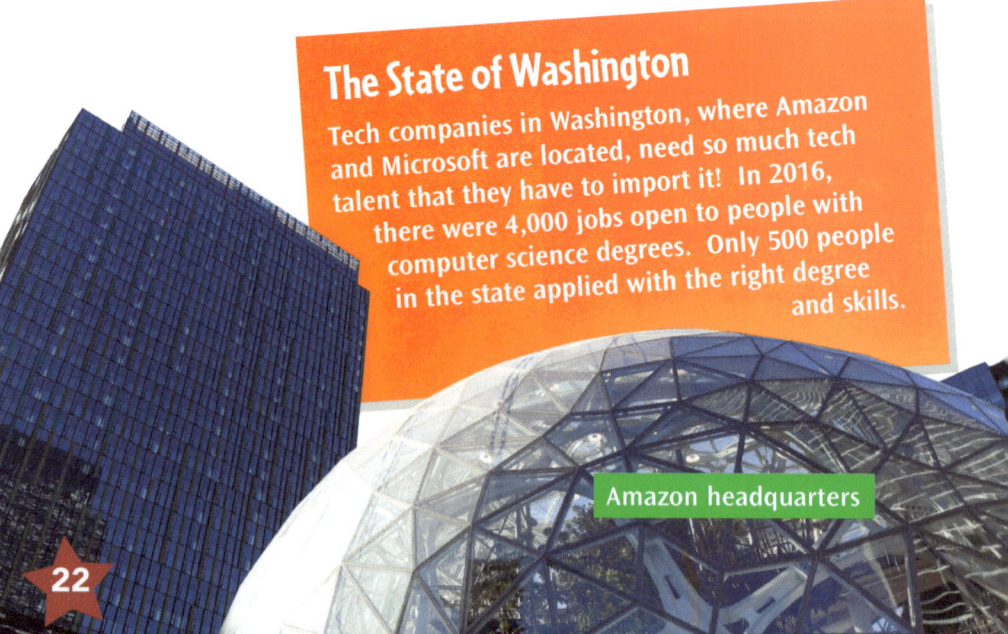

The State of Washington

Tech companies in Washington, where Amazon and Microsoft are located, need so much tech talent that they have to import it! In 2016, there were 4,000 jobs open to people with computer science degrees. Only 500 people in the state applied with the right degree and skills.

Amazon headquarters

Get-Up-And-Go

When Pan saw another student her age pitching at the Seattle Startup Weekend event in 2015, she knew it was her time. Within three days, she had made her pitch, built the app mock-up (which took her about two hours), and come up with the name iRummage. The concept ultimately took third place.

Pan at the start-up event

Watch It Grow

Seed capital is the money required to get a new business off the ground. Sometimes, the people who start the company put up the funds themselves. But friends and family—and sometimes investors—can contribute, too.

Pan presenting at Fast Pitch

The Next Phase

iRummage was **incorporated** the month after Pan first pitched the idea. But the then-12-year-old **CEO** knew she had more work to do. By the next summer, she finished the app's design with the help of a team of tech experts.

In the fall of 2016, iRummage won first place in the high school category at the Social Venture Partners Fast Pitch finals. The recognition got the app some financial support. And the coaching she received from experts also helped Pan develop her original idea further.

Since then, she has fine-tuned the app, which she hopes will raise millions of dollars for Washington schools. In the process, the schoolkids who manage the rummage sales will also learn what it's like to run a company. She even expects kids as young as first grade to play key roles in the venture. They will help collect items to sell and will get the community involved.

Really Fast Pitch

If the "Fast Pitch Final Showdown" sounds rather intense, it certainly is! Finalists have a mere five minutes to pitch their ideas to a room full of people who could help them in big ways.

Where There's a Will...

Just ahead of her Fast Pitch win, Pan was interviewed by a tech news website about what a typical day in a student-CEO's life was like. She told them that after the interview she would have to return to school to finish science class. Then, she had choir, PE, math, seminars, and finally **crew**. (She mentioned lunch, too!)

Pan's schedule has become increasingly busier as she has gotten older. But the amount she can accomplish in one day is a **testament** to her endurance and impressive **work ethic**. "She is **coxswain** in crew—it's not an easy job," says her father. Practice runs until dinnertime most weekdays, and competitions often last all day on Saturdays.

If and When

Pan realizes that there may come a time when leading iRummage is no longer **feasible**. If that happens, she has said that she'll replace herself with someone who has just as much heart for the company as she does. She wants her work to continue on.

Pan is not sure whether her musical and athletic strengths help sharpen her business skills. However, she does know that she enjoys all these pursuits so much that juggling them is her only option.

Pan presenting at Fast Pitch

The Future of Apps

Did you know that the two largest app stores sell more than four million apps combined? As more people around the world purchase smartphones, this number will continue to soar. If you like working with technology, consider building an app.

Cory Nieves

In the caption for an Instagram post, Cory Nieves wrote that he started from the bottom. The photo shows him in the early days of his cookie start-up, Mr. Cory's Cookies, selling his homemade goods from a stand. Nieves is older and wiser now, and much has happened since that picture was taken.

With hard work, support from his mother Lisa, and a lot of natural baking ingredients, Nieves has changed his life in a few years. He started selling hot chocolate near his home in New Jersey when he was six years old. He didn't do it to make money, but rather to help his mother buy a car. A car would save them a lot of time. Soon, Nieves realized that hot chocolate was only popular during the winter, so he expanded his menu with lemonade and cookies.

Guiding Light

Nieves certainly isn't one to take all the credit for his success. "My mom is one of my biggest inspirations," he says with great affection. "She's the person I look up to."

Nieves making cookies

What If?

Sometimes, life struggles motivate people to turn things around for the better. But Nieves says that even without the struggles he and his mom faced, he probably still would have become a businessperson. "Probably a CEO!" he adds.

Things Got Cooking

There was a lot of **trial and error** when Nieves and his mother first began baking. But after much taste-testing, they made a final recipe that they were sure everyone would love.

After baking a few batches, Nieves would pull a wagon full of cookies around his neighborhood. He stopped at places where there would undoubtedly be takers, such as barbershops and car dealerships. At one point, he and his mom were making and selling so many cookies that they had to upgrade to a **commercial** kitchen. "Each step we took, we learned," says Nieves.

Sweet Success

It wasn't long before the media caught a whiff of Mr. Cory's Cookies. Nieves's fashion sense and compelling story helped push his brand even further into the spotlight. Business magazines and network news stations interviewed him. He even made an appearance on *The Ellen DeGeneres Show*.

Surprise!

TV host Ellen DeGeneres likes to surprise guests with life-altering gifts. She was so impressed with Nieves that she wanted to do something to help his company. By the end of his time on the show, Mr. Cory's Cookies had a car, a new sign, and $10,000.

Real Life

Being an entrepreneur is super, but having an outlet for stress is important. During his downtime, Nieves practices double bass and krav maga, an Israeli martial art. He also likes to play golf, read, and study marketing.

Where He Stands

Throughout his journey, Nieves has not taken his success for granted. He and his mom still make sure the treats get to people who will appreciate them—not just to those who can afford them. The company donates money to hospitals and supplies cookies to fundraising events and shelters.

In the Future

Nieves has a multitude of interests and big plans. College is most definitely one of them. He has had his eye on Princeton since visiting there when he was younger. Big business? Highly likely. He envisions himself at the top of the corporate ladder at Starbucks or J. Crew. And he plans to build on his distinct sense of style. "You have to dress the part," says the fashion-conscious teenager, "and then people take you seriously."

Famous Friends

Mr. Cory, as he's known in the business world, has made some friends in high places. He has worked with a long list of brands, including Citibank, Mercedes-Benz, Pottery Barn, and TOMS. He has achieved an impressive level of fame, too; he has over 30,000 Instagram followers.

Bella Tipping

Australian teenager Bella Tipping is a seasoned traveler. She and her parents have stayed in many first-rate hotels. In 2014, Tipping realized that no travel websites asked *her* what she thought of the fold-out beds she had to sleep on. She thought it was time for kids to be consulted about their hotel stays. She decided kids should have a say.

The Kidzcationz website launched in September 2015. Tipping says that it took a while to find a web design team that both understood what she was trying to do and took her seriously. But the young CEO did not give up. Tipping was finally able to realize her vision at only 12 years old. And now, thousands of kids are registered on Kidzcationz and can safely post reviews of their travel experiences.

Think Positive

Sometimes, it feels like for every person who supports your creativity, there is another person whose primary goal is to crush it. "There are many out there who will tell you what you can't do. ...Don't listen to them! Stay away from negative people," advises Tipping.

Keep Thinking

"There are so many solutions for problems that people haven't thought of yet," says Bella Tipping. "I think about the boy who wanted bandages at a [ball] game and came up with the idea to have first-aid vending machines at games. He was recently offered millions to sell his business. That is being creative!"

Then and Now

Prior to starting Kidzcationz, Tipping never entertained the idea of owning a business. She admits that she wasn't even aware what an entrepreneur was. She was just a happy kid who liked to play with friends.

On One Condition

"My parents were never the kind of people who think that just because I was their only child, every idea I had was amazing," says Tipping. Before they agreed to help fund her idea, they wanted to see a business plan. And Tipping delivered.

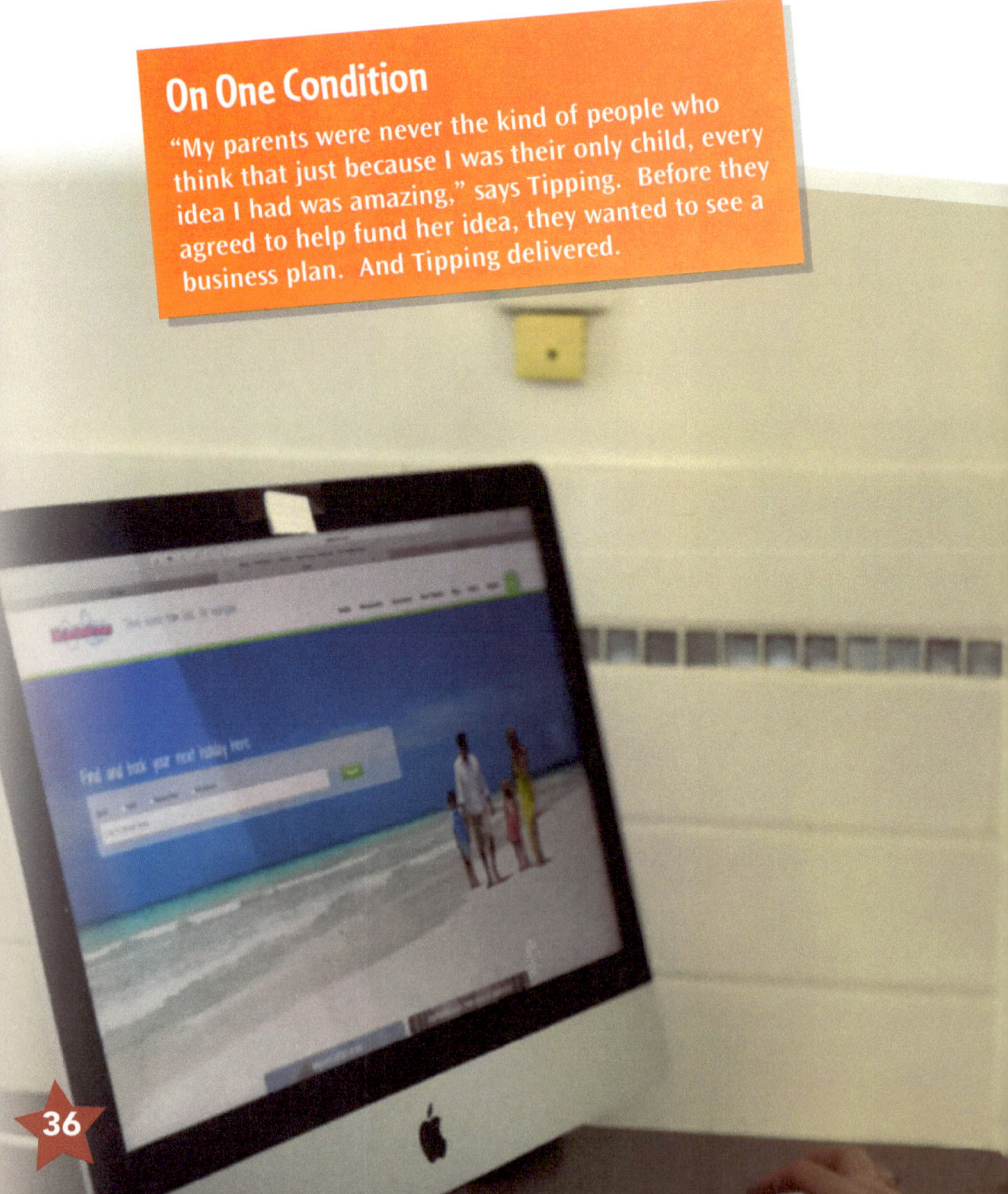

She believes that a couple **facets** of her upbringing helped her grow into her current role. As an only child, Tipping spent a good deal of time around adults and became "an active listener." She also saw a lot of grief firsthand because her parents owned a cemetery and crematorium. It gave Tipping a strong sense of how every moment matters and how important it is to treat people well.

Break Time

To truly clear her mind, Tipping reads, writes, or walks her rescue dog, Jed. She has even published a picture book called *Jed Finds His Forever Home*.

For the Greater Good

If Tipping ever opts for a different career path, she has a couple of ideas in mind. "I would love to work at Virgin Unite [the charitable arm of the Virgin Group], because **social entrepreneurship** is very important to me," she says. She also believes she would make a fine lawyer. But from the helm of Kidzcationz, Tipping works toward her goal of creating a more inclusive world.

Here are some basic differences between **commercial entrepreneurs** and social entrepreneurs:

	Commercial Entrepreneur	Social Entrepreneur
Goal	To build a business that makes a profit	To find an innovative way to make society or the world better
Risk	Often takes financial and creative risks during start-up	Often takes financial and creative risks during start-up
Meaning of Value	Positive sales projections; meeting shareholder and investor expectations	Funds that help further the cause; the contribution to society
Measure of Success	The bottom line; competitive edge; public interest	The social impact made; public involvement or support

> In what ways are commercial entrepreneurs and social entrepreneurs similar?

> Which type of business do you think would be more profitable, and why?

> Which type of business most appeals to you?

In June 2016, she started an online petition. She urged airlines to devise ways to safely lock modified wheelchairs in place on board. She was inspired to help when her uncle needed a wheelchair after an accident.

Tipping keeps getting better at taking action. "I was always the person who stood back and let everyone else go first. I was very shy and didn't draw attention to myself," she remembers. Now, she is comfortable taking a stand.

Everyone's a Critic

Tipping is better at accepting criticism than she used to be. "I have always been able to accept the word *no*, but now I understand that *no* just means *not quite*," she says about business. "It's okay to go back and have another go at something until I hear a *yes*."

The Takeaway

Takeaway is a **buzzword** for the important point everyone is supposed to learn from a meeting or other event. What is your takeaway from these stories? Are you inspired by these successful kids?

These young business owners have shown that kids have the ability to do incredible things. Because of their ages, they have unique perspectives and approaches to business issues. And they have all learned that conducting business with a **conscience** will lead to a big payoff—for everyone.

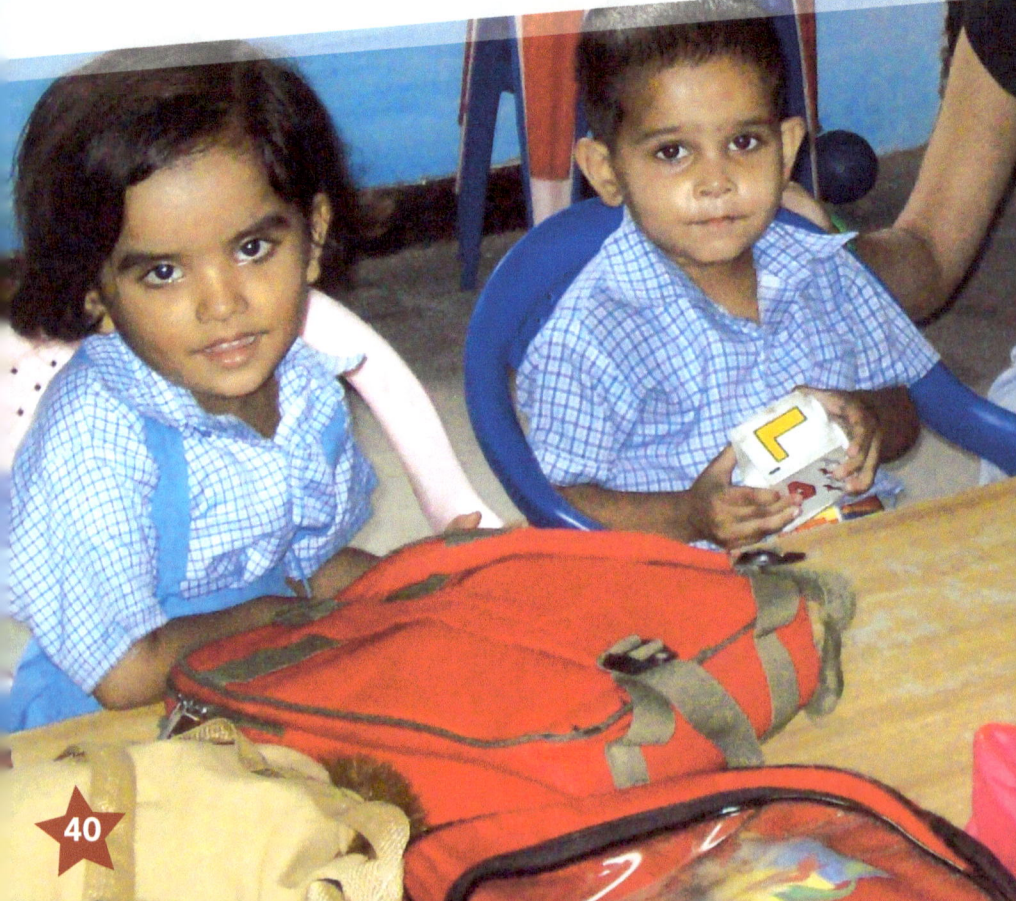

Parting Wisdom

"Life is not easy for any of us. But what of that? We must have perseverance and above all confidence in ourselves. We must believe that we are gifted for something, and that this thing, at whatever cost, must be attained."
—physicist and two-time Nobel Prize winner Marie Curie

Glossary

advocate—someone who supports a cause and/or works on behalf of others

avid—enthusiastic

buzzword—a popular word or phrase

CEO—chief executive officer, the head of a company

commercial—for the purpose of business or making a profit

commercial entrepreneurs—those who start businesses with the intention of making a profit

conscience—a feeling inside that tells you whether an action is right or wrong

coxswain—in crew, the person who steers and sets the rhythm of the rowers

crew—the sport of racing in narrow boats propelled by oars

crowdfunding—raising money for a project or business by asking a large group of people for donations

dyslexia—a learning difference that makes it difficult to read

empathy—the ability to understand and share the emotions of others

empowering—giving a sense of confidence and control, or the power to do something

entrepreneurs—people who come up with ideas for and then run businesses, especially when there is a certain amount of financial risk involved

facets—specific aspects or features of something

feasible—capable of being accomplished

fruition—the point when a goal or project is completed

groundwork—the foundation of something; the first steps that need to be accomplished

incorporated—when a company or organization becomes a legal corporation

in kind—support in the form of money, as well as goods and/or services

manpower—the supply of people available to work

pitch—to present an idea in order to sell it or gain support for it

prototype—a model or example of an original concept

sincerest—the most genuine or honest; heartfelt

social entrepreneurship—when an entrepreneur's focus is to come up with innovative ways to solve problems that impact society and then put them into effect

strides—large steps, or considerable progress

testament—evidence of something

trial and error—a method of reaching the best result by paying attention to what works and what doesn't work

upcycled—something old or thrown out that has been turned into a new product of greater value

work ethic—a set of principles governing the way something is done

Index

advocate, 18
Amazon, 22
apps, 22–23, 25, 27
Ash, Max, 6–11
Basketball Hall of Fame, 10
Boston, 6, 8
business plan, 36
charity, 9–10, 16, 38
Citibank, 33
commercial entrepreneur, 38
creativity, 7, 11, 35
crowdfunding, 9
Curie, Marie, 41
DeGeneres, Ellen, 31
downtime, 32
Durant, Kevin, 10
dyslexia, 7, 10
Ellen DeGeneres Show, The, 31
Empower Orphans, 12, 14–16
entrepreneur, 4, 11, 22, 32, 36
extracurricular activities, 18
Fenway Park, 8
fundraising, 16, 22–23
green business, 20
Gupta, Neha, 12–16, 18
Howard, Lisa, 28
Instagram, 28, 33
iRummage, 23, 25–26
J. Crew, 33
Jed Finds His Forever Home, 37
Kidzcationz, 34–36, 38
krav maga, 32
MAX'IS Creations, 7, 10
Mercedes-Benz, 33
Microsoft, 16, 22
Mr. Cory's Cookies, 28, 31
Nieves, Cory, 28–33
nonprofit, 14
Nordstrom, 10

online business, 21
Pan, Belle, 22–27
Pan, JT, 22
patent, 7
Pennsylvania State University, 18
perseverance, 41
pitch, 8, 22–27
podcast, 21
Pottery Barn, 33
Princeton University, 33
Seattle, 22–23
seed capital, 24
social entrepreneur, 38
Social Venture Partners Fast Pitch, 25
Starbucks, 33
start-up, 22–23, 28
Student, 4
The Mug With A Hoop, 8
Tipping, Bella, 34–39
TOMS, 33
Washington, 22, 25

Check It Out!

Books

Cerone, Lulu. 2017. *PhilanthroParties! A Party-Planning Guide for Kids Who Want to Give Back.* Aladdin/Beyond Words.

Jordan, Gabrielle. 2011. *The Making of a Young Entrepreneur: A Kid's Guide to Developing the Mind-Set for Success.* Legacy Builder Group, LLC.

Linecker, Adelia Cellini. 2004. *What Color Is Your Piggy Bank? Entrepreneurial Ideas for Self-Starting Kids.* Lobster Press.

MacGregor, Mariam G. 2006. *Everyday Leadership: Attitudes and Actions for Respect and Success (a Guidebook for Teens).* Free Spirit Publishing.

McGillian, Jamie Kyle. 2016. *The Kids' Money Book: Earning, Saving, Spending, Investing, Donating.* Sterling Children's Books.

Zeiler, Freddi. 2006. *A Kid's Guide to Giving.* Innovative Kids.

Websites

Empower Orphans. www.empowerorphans.org.

iRummage. www.irummage.org.

Kidzcationz. www.kidzcationz.com

MAX'IS Creations. www.maxiscreations.com.

Mr. Cory's Cookies. www.mrcoryscookies.com.

Try It!

The kids you just met have a lot of business sense. But they are only five of countless young people with brilliant ideas. We bet you have some great ideas, too! Choose one idea, and write a company description using the questions below as a guideline.

★ Describe what the business does and why it is needed.

★ How will your business fulfill this need?

★ Who are you providing products or services for? Or are you trying to help other businesses? Try to be as specific as possible.

★ What gives your business a competitive edge? Are you an expert in the field? Are you offering a product that is totally new to the market?

About the Author

Michelle R. Prather is a longtime writer and editor. She got her start interviewing business owners and telling their stories in magazines. Since then, she has written guided planners and journals, edited young adult novels, and coauthored an art book. She started college as a dance major, but she ended up with degrees in film studies and history. Her big dreams include opening the best-ever children's bookstore and writing a fiction series her daughter would love.

www.ingramcontent.com/pod-product-compliance
Lightning Source LLC
Chambersburg PA
CBHW041505010526
44118CB00001B/25